pier 1 candles:

elements of the table

CollinsPublishersSanFrancisco
A Division of HarperCollins*Publishers*

First published 1996 by
Collins Publishers
10 E. 53rd street,
New York, New York 10022
HarperCollins Web site:
http://www.harpercollins.com

Copyright©1998 Pier 1 Imports (U.S.), Inc.
Photography Copyright ©1998 Greg Booth +Assoc.
Copyright©1996 Sara Slavin and Deborah Jones
Photography Copyright ©1996 Deborah Jones
Design Copyright ©1996 Morla Design, Inc.

Book and Cover Design: Morla Design
Photo Assistants: Jerry Jones,
Sara Gummere, Virginia deCarvalho,
and Ellen Callaway

Library of Congress Cataloging-in-Publication Data:
Slavin, Sara. Candles: elements of the table /
by Sara Slavin: photography by Deborah Jones.
p. cm.
ISBN 0-00-225078-0
1. Table settings and decoration.
2. Candles. I. Title.
TX879.S5796 1996
642'.8--dc20   96-15433
                CIP

Printed in China
10 9 8 7 6 5 4 3 2

contents:

glowing

No matter how diverse, how geographically distinct the world's spiritual traditions, most share two elements—feasting and the lighting of candles. There is something so quietly ritualized about putting light to candles. The gesture says, now we may begin. From Candlemas to Kwanzaa, Dia de los Muertos to Hanukkah, candlelight casts a glow rich in meaning. In fact, candles have been part of ceremonies and celebrations for thousands of years. But candles can also be a very simple, very inexpensive way to add a note of festivity to even the most everyday of occasions. ∽∽∽∽

This book is designed to introduce some of the easiest, most lighthearted ways to use candles as part of any meal, any event. In this chapter, you'll find history and lore about candles and candle making, some classic, romantic references to candles in literature, and some unexpected ways to use them—from stately tapers to tiny votives—to create your own magic.

Sharing a meal and watching candlelight reflected in the eyes of those we care about are two pleasures that remind us of all we have in common and all we have to celebrate. Whether it's lighting a candle on a Hanukkah menorah, counting down to Christmas with Advent candles, or simply enjoying the soothing quality of candlelight, we imbue candles with a magical presence. Wax is, after all, an eminently adaptable art medium. It can be shaped (and lit) for elegance or fun.

shaped

Candles are inextricably linked to romance and lovers. It was, when all is said and done, just one candle that brought Puccini's ill-fated lovers together in *La Boheme*. When Mimi's candle goes out in her chilly attic room, she knocks on the door of her neighbor, the poet Rodolpho, to ask if her taper can be relit from his candle. He offers her a restorative sip of wine; they sit together at his humble, candlelit table — and promptly fall in love. When the light goes out one more time, Rodolpho's hand finds Mimi's, and he begins the loveliest of arias, *"Che gelida manina."* ⌒

votives

There's no rule that says candles must be inserted into candlesticks, displayed vertically, and lit all at once. Tiny, squat votives, the simplest of shapes and available in an array of colors, can contribute to a still-life, displayed by the flicker of just one small, lit candle. History has it that when the late Jacqueline Kennedy Onassis threw a bridal dinner for her sister Lee Radziwill, guests entered to find her entire home filled with glowing white votive candles. Votives of any color can be grouped on a flat, round plate, placed in the center of a table, and lit for a centerpiece that's both compelling and low enough for guests to converse across. Votives are also the perfect size for placing in unexpected holders — tiny terra-cotta pots, flat miniature pumpkins (with a hole carved in the top), lady apples, or even a collection of treasured cups and saucers. ∽

Once candles seemed like something re-
served for "Big Occasions" — two tapers
set like soldiers, flanking a mercilessly
arranged centerpiece. Today, those
seeking a little grace find creative
ways to integrate candles and the
warm light they conjure into everyday

lingerir

flicker

life. There's something wonderfully extravagant about a pleasure that is literally used up at a sitting. You know it's a terrific dinner party when the guests are still lingering at the table as the candles flicker and burn very, very low. Fortune candles, with little silver or gold charms or rolled-up fortunes embedded inside, are perfect ways to end the evening. Guests wait until the wax melts to reveal the fortune — and then claim them for their own.

candlelight

On our tables, candles cast the loveliest of lights.
Everything — and everyone — looks better by candlelight.
The gentle character of the light changes even the
most ordinary of settings and occasions into something
quite special. Elizabeth Barrett Browning observed
the transforming quality of candlelight in her poem
The Lady's Yes: "'Yes,' I answered you last night:/
'No,' this morning sir, I say:/ Colors seen by candle-
light/ Will not look the same by day." Candles are
transforming, no doubt about it, which may help account
for their inextricable link to romance as well. ⌒

Candlemaking has a long and complex history. There's no clear evidence of the "invention" of a candle, but candleholders were discovered in both ancient Cretan ruins (1600 B.C.E.) and in King Tut's tomb (14th century B.C.E.). The word *candle* has a luminous origin – from the Latin *candere*, meaning to shine. By the 13th century, candlemakers had their own guild and, in France, traveled village to village, house to house to make candles. Paraffin, derived from the petroleum seeps of Derbyshire, came into widespread use in the 19th century as a substitute for the more expensive beeswax.

celebrations

On the ecclesiastical calendar, the festival of
Candlemas has been celebrated since the 11th century.
The holiday falls on February 2, when bleak winter has
not yet given way to spring — and the light of the
candles seems especially welcome. On that day, candles
are blessed to commemorate the presentation of the
infant Jesus in the Temple and the purification of the
Virgin Mary. In early renaissance paintings of the
Annunciation, we often find Mary reading by candlelight when the Angel comes to call.

Many other cultural traditions incorporate candles
as well. Kwanzaa, a modern-day celebration that
commemorates the African harvest of the first fruits
of the year, is observed for seven nights and the
holiday table is set with a straw mat, a candle holder
for seven red, green, and black candles, and fruits
and vegetables. In Mexico, the *Dia de los Muertos*, the

Day of the Dead, is a yearly festival that brings the spirits of lost loved ones back for a gala feast. Candles are lit to mark the way for returning spirits and scattered throughout the *ofrenda*, a fanciful altar that unites food, flowers, clothing, and photographs for the spirits to enjoy during their short visit on earth.

Wherever Christmas is celebrated, candles occupy a place of honor. The Irish put lighted candles in the windows on Christmas Eve to create a path of light for the Christ child. In England and France, Christmas Eve dinner lasted as long as the grand, oversized Yule candle kept burning. For Swedes, the vision of Christmas is the candlelit wreath of leaves worn by a young woman in honor of Saint Lucia. Wreaths featuring four candles, one for each week of Advent, originated in Germany and are now part of many cultures' traditions. (Lavender, the color of penitence, is the usual color for the candles, but some families use one pink candle to symbolize hope and celebration for the third Sunday in Advent.) ➢

Simple and pure in shape and color, a classic white or cream candle can take on all the beautifully Protean qualities of "the little black dress." Candles adapt and enhance a myriad of containers — from crystalline candleholders to antique silver sticks to holders simply appropriated for the purpose of centering a

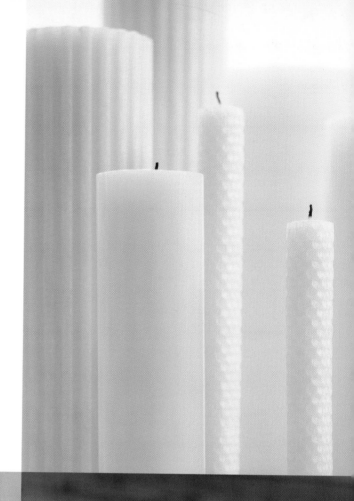

hold **create** a unifying feeling. Little wonder that silver is a classic material for candlesticks. The flicker of candlelight, reflected in the highly polished surface of silver, creates both drama and **intimacy** on a table. The more baroque and elaborate the stick, the more pared-down and simple the candle should be.

beautiful, flickering light. Surround a fat column stick with fragrant herb leaves — aromatic bay, fresh rosemary studded with lavender, pink or blue flowers, a wreath of fragrant thyme. Group a mini-collection of holders — different heights, shapes, and proportions — and watch as the **candles** they

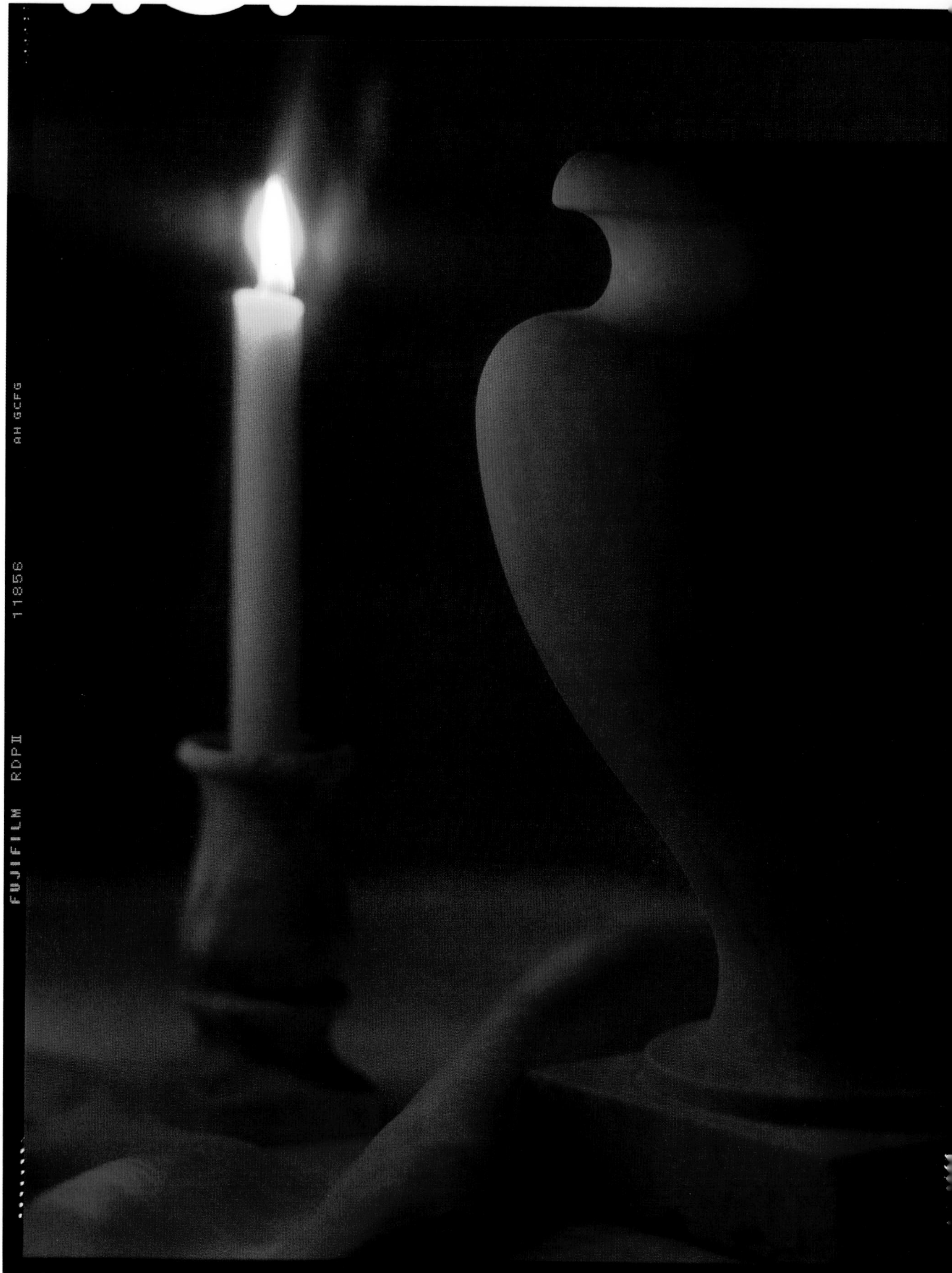
FUJIFILM RDP II
11856
AH GCFG

spirit

Candles are multicultural guardians against darkness and despair. The Roman goddess Vesta, charged with watching over hearth and home, was worshiped in a temple that kept a perpetual flame. Both Greeks and Romans used burning candles at funerals to keep wicked spirits from seizing the soul of their loved one. In Greece, Turkey, and part of Spain, "grandfather" candles, made of entwined threads, are burned from the first Monday of Lent until Pentecost in honor of deceased grandparents. Each thread honors the memory of a lost loved one. ⌣

silvery style

Silversmithing, the art and craft of turning *argentum* into objects, has a decorative and functional history. Silver objects, designed for both domestic and ceremonial use, date back to the 5th century B.C.E. and are treasured artifacts from India, South America, and virtually all European civilizations. Paul Revere was a silversmith who turned his skill in casting weaponry to more artistic purposes after the Revolution — and is considered a founding father of the clean lines of American-made silver objects. Today's silver artists still find a happy marriage between silver's lustrous look and candles' warm light. The stylized lines of the Scandinavian artist-jewelers like Georg Jensen elevate everyday objects to rare and collectible status. The twist of a beautiful candlestick sets off the pure verticality of a simple taper. Whether silver is burnished to a high gleam, or slightly gentled in shine by age, it provides a perfect setting for the luminous glow of candlelight. ⌒

Chiaroscuro is what painters call the use of light and shade in sculpting what we see. The magic of candles— large, small, contained in glass, or flickering in the open—can turn the table into a canvas, ready for the drama and mystery that candlelit chiaroscuro can invent. Best of all, as the candles burn low, the balance of light to shadow will change, creating a rhythm to the evening.

t h e a t e r

Candlelight creates a theatrical set, plunging a room into alternating patterns of light and shadow. It comes as no surprise that the first indoor theater illumination was by candles. When actors came to acknowledge the audience at the footlights, they had to take care that the sweep of their bows did not set wig or costume aflame. In *Romeo and Juliet*, when Shakespeare, referred to the fading stars, wrote "night's candles are burnt out," his audience was quite accustomed to imagining the flickering of candles as virtually the only light an imagination could need.

collectibles

32 Candlesticks have much to recommend them as collectibles. They range in value from priceless, treasured by the great auction houses and housed in museums, to heirlooms, handed down in families, to serendipitous tag sale finds. But, unlike some collectibles that live a sterile existence, backlit on a display shelf, candlesticks can be put to everyday use. Georgian silver, folk art handicrafts, art school projects, ceramic sculptures, pewter wedges — candleholders reflect the art, vision, taste, and raw materials of their maker. On a mantel, on a sideboard, and of course, on the table, candleholders provide a way to marry form to function with everyday beauty. ⌒

materials

Unless you indulge in the luxury of beeswax, most candles are made from paraffin, with a little stearin added to reduce dripping. Paraffin replaced tallow in the mid-19th century as the preferred raw material—it is colorless, and odorless, and it burns easily. Wicks are generally made of braided cotton and, when ready to be lit, should be kept trimmed to no more than an inch in length. Wax perfumes, formulated specifically for use in candle making, can add fragrance from subtle to heady. Scented candles generally work best outside a dining room where their fragrance won't compete with the appetizing aromas wafting from the table. Of course, nothing clears a kitchen of unpleasant cooking odors more effectively than a burning candle.

Beeswax is the most prized material for candles, both for aesthetic and historical reasons. The fine honeycomb texture of the wax, the slow burn, the clean aroma, all add to the beauty of the candle. But originally, beeswax was valued because of the pagan belief that bees were messengers from paradise. The souls of the dead came back to earth as bees, highly prized and useful greetings from the world beyond. In the Middle Ages, beeswax was accepted as payment of debt. Wax-makers developed stamps to certify that what they were producing was pure beeswax, unadulterated with tallow. Beeswax candles are still the most expensive, but they are things of beauty — and burn with a luxurious leisure. ⌒·

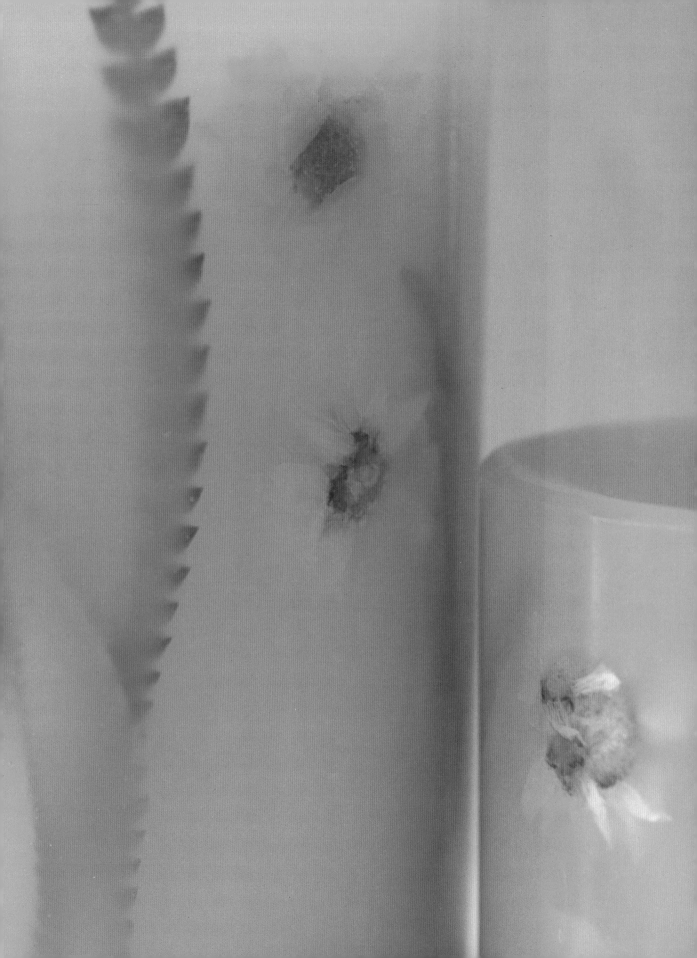

enhanced

How to enhance an already perfect gift? Consider a lightly scented candle, all dressed up for presentation with the addition of luxurious satin or organdy ribbon and a few silk flowers. Or choose a plain column candle and use raffia to tie on a few sprigs of aromatic rosemary or one just-picked, long-lasting gardenia or camellia.

The art of enhancing candles can turn the simple into the spectacular. In this chapter, you'll discover ideas to enhance candles for gift giving, new and unconventional ways to use containers, and a collection of customs that link candles to traditional celebrations. Most of these ideas require very little time to put together, and rely only on your own ability to see familiar objects in a brand-new light.

A gift of candles is a gift of light, warmth, smoke and dreams, and magic, magic, magic.

What to bring for dinner?
Wine...always nice, but a
shade too expectable. Flowers...
a little too much for the
host or hostess to fuss with
at the last minute. Candy...
all those calories! How about
candles? A beautiful beehive
of beeswax, adorned with a
lush ribbon. A gathering of
pastel tapers captured in a
luxurious napkin. A jump-
start on spring with a tiny
pot, a seed-packet, and a
perfect candle. A cellophaned,
fluted firecracker, gathered
in a topknot and adorned with
a regal label. ⌢

tableaux

Weary of the same old flowers-plus-candles in the center of the table? Ahhhh... imagination. Candles lend themselves to all sorts of creative tableaux — placed at random in a still-life of miniature furniture, set high and low on stacks of beloved books, studded like sparkling gems in entwining wreaths of ivy or grapevine. Picture tiny lights glowing in the windows of a child's dollhouse at a birthday party or tea. Create tier upon tier of lit candles on plates set on a three-story pie safe. Float candles on a tabletop pond of water in a beautiful bowl. Stage a candlelit dessert buffet on a sideboard, and watch what flickering lights can do to the glisten of lemon tarts and the sparkle of frosted grapes. ✍

Candles can be cast in a mold, dipped, or poured. The charm of molded candles is that virtually any object can be used as a mold — from a simple milk carton to any "found" container that can hold wax. Round molds — from blown eggshells to Christmas ornaments — turn out wonderfully globelike candles. These intriguing "narrative" candles were created by lining carton molds with yesterday's news from a local Chinatown paper and a child's assignment sheet from school. The result? Meltable art that integrates language and light in one consumable medium. ⌀

molding

"But then they danced down the
street...the ones who never
yawn or say a commonplace thing,

but burn, burn, burn like
fabulous yellow roman candles."

Jack Kerouac, *On the Road*

Marble garden ornaments or antique stone pedestals lend a certain

48   altarlike formality to a grouping of candles. Light at 15-minute

intervals and you'll create an interestingly staggered group of flames

Folk traditions have it that when candle flames snap or burn unevenly, there's bad weather coming. Of course, encasing candles in glass is one guardian against the exigencies of weather. Hurricane lamps, tall, sturdy, **glass-enclosed** lights that shelter the flame and enhance the glow, were

developed as practical solution to the flicker-turned-gus problem. But even indoors, th magic created when a flame glow inside glass is as aesthetic a it is practical. Glass enhance and amplifies the power of th **flame**, reflecting a glo on all it lights. There's an other functional side to glass

obeche, the thin glass disk
laced between candle and can-
lestick, protects the stick from
ripping, melting wax. Romantics
ave compared the sight of a
andle glowing inside glass to
he **mystery** of a woman's
ace behind a veil. Like a veil,
he glass both obscures and
nlarges the power of what is

seen inside. Candles inside
glass also have powerful reli-
gious significance. Jews remem-
ber the anniversary of a beloved
family member's passing
by lighting a *yahrzeit*, a small
candle contained in a glass.
Once lit, the candle is never
extinguished, it simply burns
until it flickers and goes out.

unexpected

Part of the artistry of seeing
candles anew is being willing
to marry container to candle,
setting to table, with a fresh
eye. Beloved objects, whatever
their original use, need to
come out of breakfronts and
boxes and remind us why we
take pleasure in them. Gather
simple lightweight twists
of creamy candles and arrange
them in a silver baby cup. Set
match to wicks, and watch as
the candles burn in a casual
trio, melting down as the evening progresses and casting new
shadows on a festive table. ⌒

52

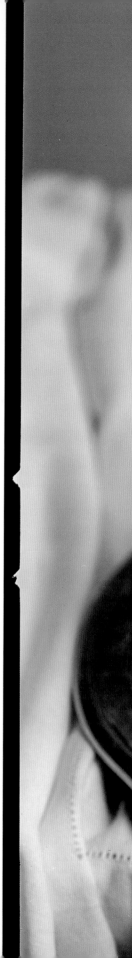

Lights on a Christmas tree are simply

a safe way to recapture the magical

look of the traditional candelit tree.

The custom of putting candles on a

tree supposedly comes from the Protes-

tant reformer Martin Luther. Luther

is said to have been inspired when he

was walking through a pine woods

one winter evening and caught sight

of a starry sky twinkling through

the canopy of trees.

We credit Mexico for the invention of luminarias, beautiful improvised candleholders made from paper bags. Each bag is scissored to create simple cutout designs, then the bottom quarter filled with sand to weigh it down. The top of the bags are rolled down to create a cuff, and a glass candleholder and candle put inside. Like little glowing soldiers, lines of luminarias light walkways, patios, even winter beaches on Christmas Eve. ⌁

on-screen

The warm light that candles cast creates a distinctive mood. Perhaps that's why director Stanley Kubrick chose to light so much of his lush film *Barry Lyndon* with real candles. The result was a visual feast, with 18th-century England looking exceptionally opulent and touchable. The interior shots, from dining hall to bath scene, were shot by candlelight — Thackeray never looked so enticing. Oscars for best art direction, set direction, cinematography, and costume design were awarded — a testament to the rich flattery of candlelit scenes. You can set an immediate mood of festive intimacy by filling your entryway with candles. Guests enter to the soft glow of candlelight, a sure sign of a magical evening ahead. ⌒

impromptu

Antique Regency candlesticks a
terrific to have, but the fact
the matter is...virtually any co
tainer can be put to use as

intriguing candleholde

Take a tour through a restaura
supply store, or cruise throu
your own cupboards. Heavy jel
jars, French bistro glasses, sh
glasses, baking tins, tartlet pan

ny tin or copper molds — all

ese can hold candles from

alight size on up. And, don't

rry if the wax melts and pud-

es. A round-edged wooden spoon

a plastic credit card can make a

eat, nonscratch scraper. Wash

th warm, soapy water and your im-

romptu candleholders

e ready for service once again.

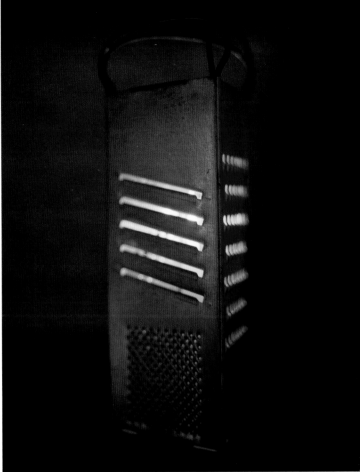

ideas

Kitchen cupboards are full of inspiration. Consider a flat-bottomed old wooden bowl holding one fat candle, rings of votive candles on a three-tiered cake pedestal, a heavy cast-iron skillet holding candles of many **different** sizes for a charmingly rustic look. Antique cans or tins can be hole-punched to become candleholders. Stack white bistro plates high to hold a simple, substantial white candle. Place an antique scale in the middle of the table with candles on both sides. Remove the tops from salt and pepper shakers — and they're ready-made, **whimsical** candlesticks. And don't overlook the classic Chianti bottle. Something about it just cries out for a **wonderful**, drippy, melting candle. Finally, picture a late-night comfort supper, with scrambled eggs, home-fried potatoes, and warm, fragrant blueberry muffins. Tea towels serve as bistro-style napkins, and in the center of the table, a collection of muffin liners, each one featuring a glowing votive. Put a little vintage Patsy Cline or Billie Holiday on the stereo — and toast the evening.

generous gifts

A thank-you gift of candles invites creativity and reminds your host or hostess how much you enjoyed the evening. Begin with fine beeswax candles, then roll them in distinctive metallic or textured paper, add some cellophane, and tie up the package with elegant ribbon. Or, extend the candle theme to the wrapping by securing brown craft paper with sealing wax. Customize with the recipient's name written on the paper with a gold- or silver-ink pen or choose a favorite quote — about candles, hospitality, or friendship — to inscribe along the side of the paper. Add a grace note with an exotic box or pretty tin of matches. Or, if the recipient is a movie buff, add a video of a movie featuring candles — David Niven in *Candleshoe,* for instance.

birthdays

One lovely variation on the birthday candle custom

comes from the Germans. When some German children are

christened, a traditional gift to commemorate the

occasion is a "twelve-year candle." From top to bottom,

the candle is marked with twelve milestones. Then,

each year on the child's birthday, the candle is burned

to the next mark. Giving such a candle — which you

can create by pouring in a marked mold or by enhancing

a pillar candle yourself — along with a specially

monogrammed cup or candleholder reflects the giver's

interest in staying involved in the child's life. ❧

Happy Birthday! What a creative way to celebrate a 40th (or any other) birthday...with an overflowing box that collects 40 candles in various sizes, shapes, and colors. Add a box of matches and the celebrant will be ready for any occasion. Associating candles with birthdays has many reported origins. Medieval Christians put a taper in the hands of a child being baptized. The custom of putting candles on a birthday cake can be credited to the Germans, who began the tradition of birthday parties with their *Kinderfeste*. Greeks and Romans believed that the flame from a taper would carry their requests directly to the gods, a likely source for our practice of making a wish before blowing out the candles. Creative gift-givers can wrap a "granted wish" around candles — for a special evening; tickets to a concert, or a gift certificate for a desired treasure — and simply present them with the cake. ꙮ

w i s h

placed

Bell, book, and candle are the magic-maker's traditional tools. There is some interior sorcery that happens when candles are placed so that they light, warm, and enchant the places we gather. Sometimes it's the marriage of a single element of nature—a solitary, perfect spring lily-of-the-valley, say—brought indoors and then shown off by candle-light. Sometimes, it's a profusion of tiny candles, entwined with fresh-cut ivy vines and a spill of rose petals, to herald a special, romantic dinner. In this chapter, we explore some of the ways in which the right candle (or can-dles) adds the perfect, finishing touch to any environment. You'll find grand candelabra, more holidays, ways to move candles beyond the table and onto every surface in the house, and a few ideas for lighting up the out-of-doors. It all adds up to placing candles wherever taste and oppor-tunity create the perfect spot.

Sometimes less is not more, more is more. Candles can create such an opulent mood when they are used in profusion. A grand table and a grand occasion call for a little extravagance. Why stop at just two lavish cande-labra when you can scatter small votives in silver holders up and down the table? The intimacy of the small lights offsets the formality of the branched candleholders and brings the table together. Guests lean close to each other, sharing toasts, confidences, and good company in a shared pool of light. ⌣

"O, how full of briers is this working-day world!"

74

It's Friday night, it's been

the longest week on record,

it's time to order in Chinese,

turn out the lights in the

kitchen and dining room, and

move to more relaxed quarters.

Funny how even a well-used

room can take on new character

when you kick off your shoes,

dim the lights, throw cushions

on the floor, and cast a mood

with colorful candles. ⌒

relax

arts & crafts

In the 18th century, a pure, waxy substance from the head of the sperm whale was used for candlemaking. The unit of measure we call "candlepower" springs from those early spermaceti candles. One candlepower is equivalent to the light given by one pure spermacetic candle — weighing one-sixth of a pound, and burning at 120 grams per hour. Many of the loveliest antique lamps were designed to hold one or more long-burning candles. The warm light they cast through delicate, translucent shades creates a surprising amount of candlepower. Small reading and piano lamps of the Victorian era, handmade pieces from the Arts and Crafts movement, jewelrylike miniatures, all created gemlike settings in which candles provided a warm light from within. ∽

There's no reason to wait for night to fall to light the candles. The gloom of winter can be dispelled with a collection of forcing bulbs, flanked by glowing candles in the window ledge. Both blossoms and lights are harbingers of spring, a promise of hope and renewal. In fact, candles can be wonderful vehicles for blurring the boundaries between indoors and outdoors. Carve pumpkins, squashes, and gourds into casual candleholders. Wrap tapers or column candles in vining leaves. Press fresh flower petals onto candles, or dry pansies in silica gel and attach the brightly colored preserved blooms with a small amount of melted wax glue. You can protect these "botanicals" with a dip into a can of molten paraffin for a final coat.

Of all the holidays associated with candles, perhaps none is more joyous than Hanukkah, the Festival of Lights. Unlike the more solemn High Holidays of the Jewish calendar, Hanukkah is really a wonderful children's party. It commemorates the heroic battle of the Maccabees, who against all odds triumphed over Antiochus Epiphanes in the year 165 B.C.E., and were able to rededicate the Temple at Jerusalem. The Shammes candle is used to light a new candle on each of the eight nights of Hanukkah, beginning with one the first night, and on through the last night. Music, games, and the consumption of great, delicious piles of latkes, or potato pancakes, follow the lighting of the candles. ∾∾∾∾∾

Candles figure in many nursery rhymes. "Jack be nimble/Jack be quick/Jack jump over the candlestick." We have Mick Jagger to

thank for the updated version of the rhyme with the irresistible "Jumpin' Jack Flash." And Mother Goose's personification of

the candle: "Little Nanny Etticoat / In a white petticoat, / and a red nose; / The longer she stands / the shorter she grows."

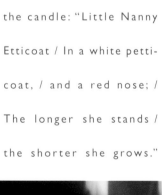

Is there a proper place for candles?
Anywhere, everywhere. Many people know the
pleasures of escaping the stresses
of a long day with a bath by candlelight.
And, of course, candles always have a
place on the table. But where else? Think
about candles in wall sconces, candles on
entry tables, on sideboards and buffets.
Consider clearing the coffee table of every
book, every magazine, every potted plant
and creating a ravishing still-life of dozens
of candles in glass holders — all in
the same color family, but composed of every

size and shape imaginable. Consider adapting

a chandelier so that it holds glowing

candles instead of lightbulbs. Collect folk

art lanterns from other cultures — in tin,

filigreed iron, aluminum, they make simple,

colorful light-bearing vessels to place

on outdoor tables or hang in trees. And, if

there's a little citronella in the candles

you use outdoors, you'll help dissuade insects

from joining the party. Candles create

an environment, wherever they are — softer,

friendlier, more festive. ✎

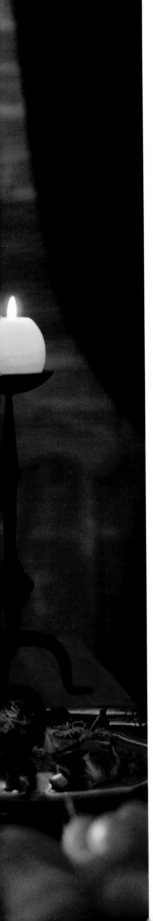

time & place

Romantics call Paris the City of Light, and perhaps that is why an entirely candlelit dining room seems to have a certain *je ne sais quoi*. Candles, candles everywhere, and not a light-bulb in sight. From the candlelit wall sconces to the artfully random collection of tapers at various heights on the table, the entire room is gently luminous. With draperies cloaking the window and eliminating ambient light from the out-of-doors, the dining room is transformed into a kind of dramatic cave or wine cellar. Guests lose all track of pedes-trian time and place, and are held captive in a never-never land of the perfect dinner party.

Though candles are an ancient form of
illumination, they can set a stage as
up-to-the-minute as today's headlines.
When art nouveau burst upon the scene in
the late 19th and early 20th centuries,
its fresh look drew inspiration not from
the past, but from the flowing, sinuous
lines in nature. Those wavy shapes that
broke free from the heavy ornamentation

of the Victorians lightened the look
of homes. A streamlined modern table,
set with tapers that emerge from nouveau-
style curving lines, a second tier of
modest candles illuminating the spaces
in between — all combine to paint an
environment that refreshes with its sim-
plicity. A little Faure or Satie on
the stereo and it's a setting that cele-
brates what was new when our grandparents
were young. ⌒

twilight

When night begins to fall, light branch-hung candle lamps

and fall in love with the quiet blessings of nature.

"Far-swooping elbow'd earth — rich apple-blossom'd earth!/

Smile, for your lover comes" (Walt Whitman, *Song of Myself*).

Candles are as ancient as a Greek ruin and as up-to-the-

minute as a late 20th century café. They are the friend-

liest, most accessible of indulgences, just waiting for a

match and the right moment. Votives and tealights, tapers

and columns, polished silver candelabra and thick French

jelly jar glasses. Candles, containers, settings, and a

spark of imagination — let the light begin. ✍

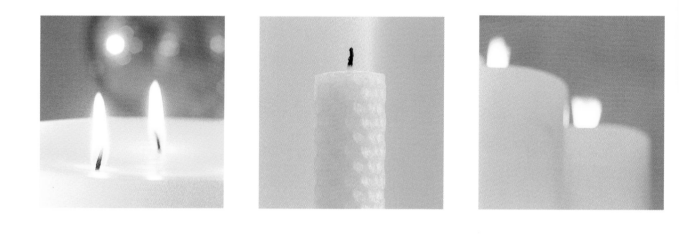

by:

Sara Slavin

and

Deborah Jones

photographs:

Greg Booth + Associates

Deborah Jones

art direction & styling:

Pier 1 imports

Sara Slavin

text:

Linda Peterson

design:

Morla Design

a c k n o w l e d g e m e n t s :

It is a pleasure to express our deep gratitude and appreciation to the following people, whose generosity, support, and creativity contributed so enormously to this book. And so we acknowledge:

Jenny Barry, who created this series and gave us the opportunity to produce it.

Jennifer Morla, Petra Geiger, and the staff at Morla Design for giving the photos and words form, spirit, and style.

Linda Peterson for her glowing words that married photography and design, and who told this story with knowledge, poetry, humor, and grace.

Jennifer Ward, Maura Carey Damacion, and the staff at Collins Publishers San Francisco for their trust, enthusiasm, and support.

K.D. Sullivan for great and swift copyediting.

Jerry Jones,photo assistant extraordinaire, for her diligence and gracious spirit.
As well, we acknowledge:

Pier 1 imports for concept, art direction and styling of unique Pier 1 merchandise.

Greg Booth + Associates for their inspiring translation of Pier 1 lifestyle through photography.

bibliography:

Newman, Thelma R. <u>Creative Candlemaking</u>, Crown
Publishers, 1972.

Nussle, William. <u>Candle Crafting</u>, Barnes, 1971.

Osborne, Harold, editor. <u>The Oxford Companion to the
Decorative Arts</u>, Oxford at the Clarendon Press, 1975.

Reader's Digest, <u>Crafts & Hobbies</u>, The Reader's Digest
Association, 1979.

Rinkoff, Barbara. <u>Birthday Parties Around the World</u>,
M. Barrows and Company, Inc., 1967.

Webster, William E. <u>Contemporary Candlemaking</u>,
Farm Journal, 1972.

credits: